Nowhere to Go
but Everywhere

Travel Poems

Milenko (Miles) Budimir

ROADSIDE PRESS

Nowhere to Go but Everywhere:
Travel Poems
Copyright © Milenko Budimir 2026
ISBN: 979-8-9996256-5-6

Editor: Michele McDannold
Cover, Interior and Back Cover Photography: Milenko Budimir

Roadside Press
Meredosia, Illinois

Table of Contents

Introduction

My first memory—I'm 3 years old. I'm in a large cavernous space; an airport somewhere in the U.S. or Europe. Taking my first international trip to visit the land of my ancestors, Yugoslavia, with my parents, who had immigrated to the United States in the 1960s.

My father loved to tell tales of his time in the JNA (the *Jugoslovenska Narodna Armija*), the Yugoslav People's Army, barely a decade on from the slaughter of WWII in that unhappy country. He traveled all across that land, and had a story from seemingly every town and city, hamlet and region.

And so, the die was cast. And likely where my own love affair with travel comes from—to scratch the itch of finding some new "over there."

Especially in these times, parochialism just won't do. In these darkening days of growing suspicion of migrants and immigrants, the push to close borders and limit cultural exchanges, threatening to place even more barriers between people, the freedom to travel and experience the world must be asserted and celebrated.

Travel is more important than ever —whether forced, as the timeless routes of refugees and migrant movements, or the travels of we the privileged.

Our collective survival depends on it—broadening, not narrowing, our worlds. Protesting the growing darkness around us and asserting the primacy of light and love, of exploration and discovery, both of the wider world and of our own common humanity.

—Milenko Budimir
December 2025

Semis speed along
asphalt ribbons, kicking up
leaves in twilight

X

Cheyenne

Eyes
dark as acid pits
that scald my bones
and boil the pillowy
marrow,
to lay beside you
this night in
this moist air
of our twilight.

Zephyr
Nebraska

Out
in that
vast open country

it

howls and roars
through tall grasses,
thuds across
open prairie,

slices through
ground clouds,
laps
unseen horizons,

reminds you
how gods
long thought dead
can live
again.

The City

Nietzsche the Swiss watch
salesman and

the holy Sikh man
selling lipstick whores
on Madison Avenue

bales of garbage
burst meat dreams

but ain't that America!

eight million people
and still
I am all
alone.

On the Subway

Oh eyes,
where to fix
on this subterranean slog:
at the canvas bag
stuffed with bags and more bags
at the multicolored subway map
above your angelic head
at your scuffed black heels
at the holy Qur'an to my left,
its fluid script dancing on the page
at the restaurant review
in *The New Yorker* to my right
at the ads lining the subway car
like ceiling molding
at your darting blue eyes
playing with mine
at your departing Russian accent

of *excuse me*
your *garbled mumble mumble...*
your back pack!...
Fuck You
at your headphone-covered ears,
bobbing and mouthing angry
anthems
          or
back at your soft delicate hands
holding your mystery book;
between Union Square and
Columbus Circle
we have made love a thousand
different ways,
been to Europe and back
a dozen times,
fought and been apart and back
together again,
watched fireworks in the harbor,
rode the Cyclone at Coney Island,

and before I know it, you are
walking out of my life
forever,
as I am warned yet again to
stand clear of the closing doors,
please.

Vieux Carré

These stormy orange streets
with a mumble and a shuffle
and a *lagniappe* hustle,
they'll take your money and run
like a bad moon rising and
a lady named Katrina'll cut
your heart out
and when the saints
oh when those saints
oh when those sweaty one-eyed saints
come marchin' in?
Oh Lady, oh Lord,
they'll pick your pockets
to feed your soul.

Before 9/11
Chicago

Bella Rada,
a Bulgarian restaurant,
and a Polish video store
on a street with
people scattering
after workers
hit a water main line better
than a gas line
and Tito Puente
swingin' on
sweet asphalt and
hot leather and
who knew that a poet laureate
lived in Oak Park
a half-pound grilled at
Michael's beef house

it's 92 degrees and 4:30
and I'm leavin' Chicago
for my
hometown

Breakfast at a Boston McDonald's (April 1999)

like the guy who invented
the frisbee, now
there's a quick way
to make a million bucks, yeah
I wish I would've
thought of that, yeah
those fuckin' red sox lost again, hey
what's this, where's the beef? you know,
we need to go in there and take him out
and saddam hussein too, yeah
that fucker needs to go, he
needs to go

Filling up in Wheeling, WV

Loud cars, pick-up trucks, fill the town's patchwork roads. People smoking. At the gas station, I find a can of Kodiak in the windshield washer fluid basin. These mountain valleys are not packed with tourists but with people of the land. The survivors. Like the woman who pulled up behind me and is in and out quicker than I am—putting enough gas in her old car to just keep it moving. Just enough.

Just enough. That could be everything here. You, me, these Appalachian flowers. We could name this place; to get by, to keep your wits about you, to not implode, collapse, sink into the fertile ground hungry to devour and replenish.

We could have everything here. Love, even.

Enough.

Jesus Loves You
Pittsburgh

Jesus loves you! Spread the word!
yes, but sometimes we doubt...
Oh but we know that's the devil
was the lesson
from the post office
this morning
which didn't occur to me
nor the doubting man in leather
in line for a book of stamps—
so I figure I shoot the
yellow painted steel
of the 7th Avenue bridge,
enjoying a sunny blue-skied
there and back
through still snowy hills and valleys,
just in time for chicken and bacon

stapled with a toothpick
and unraveled
like marriages of distant people
preoccupied with crying babies
and
crises of the midlife kind
which not even a coffee
at Java Joe's
could fix
except to tell them all
Jesus loves you

Three-Day, Pittsburgh

Three in the morning
in the old Steel City,
leaning against the '50s fridge
in a dank walk-up,
body heat,
the July moon,
a red dress,
clapping, whistles,
accordion, *tamburitza*,
the walls pulse
energy—
we are in love
with the night.

Austin, Texas

"Jose loves Jesus"
his black t-shirt
reminds us all

*Will that be all for you
today,* he asks, carrying
a tree of mini Kellogg's cereals

while Al the cabbie spots my
Midwest drawl,
his Cubs jersey
gives him away—

*Money does that
to a place*, he says,
*makes it more neurotic,
less Bohemian; it's what*

happens when people from
New York and L.A.
move in

So he's off next week
to look for
peace of mind.
I say good bye,
echo that Midwest
baseball mantra:
Keep the faith, I say,
there's always
next year!

Ode to the Hermit Crab
Mexico

Small wonder,
sideways glancer,
keeper of the flame
hiding in plain
sight,
friend from ancient days;

friend—
I envy your
secrets, wound tight
in your hard fortress;

friend,
fellow traveler,
survivor—
I am coming
for your shell.

Korea Haiku

colossus of Seoul,
hiss of market frying pans
moonless July night.

smiling Buddha grace—
kimchee pots fermenting in
monastery yard.

afternoon monsoon
mist rises from hot asphalt
green mountains exhale.

The Traveler

I.

He is hurtling through the atmosphere, high above the French Alps, slowly descending toward Milan. Through the small rounded windows daylight enters from outside. The sun is strong and bright. The cabin fills with anticipation. Boisterous Italians are shuffling about, putting their shoes back on, adjusting their watches. Soon, he'll be on the ground in the vast and surreal airport city. He will pay far too much for a cup of espresso and a pastry. He will hear delicate, feminine voices proclaim in Italian that the passengers for Alitalia flight number 781 to Prague should report to their gate for boarding. Women in impossibly high heels will scuffle past him, racing to their gate.

II.

Here, it is a hot, humid day. She attends a lecture by a noted Austrian architect on the global phenomenon of shrinking cities. His English is very good. He is from Graz. She notes his Arian features; the receding hairline, the strong Germanic cheekbones, the jutting jaw. She imagines him as an SS officer. Stern, mechanical, efficient. He likes fine cigars and delicate Viennese pastries. Well past midnight she drives home, listening to old scratchy jazz on the radio. A deer crosses the road in front of her. At home, a rabbit squats on the back lawn. She sees his large, dark eyes studying the night. Neither of them moves. An airplane flies high overhead.

Sarajevo
For Tanja

What can I offer you,
dull pearl in
your shell of eternal granite,

with your muezzin calls
and peeling bells,
your tattered hagaddah
and shepherd Vlachs

your pearly white
grave markers lining the hillsides
like spilled dragon's teeth

tired of
new beginnings

tired of the assassin's language,
his mesmerizing poetry,
the waltz of death,

displaced bit actors
in dreams of madmen
eyes as blue as
a Bosnian winter,
words as smooth as silk

from which
we weave
many-colored scarves
or red and yellow and green,
balm for your
beautiful wounds.

Four Balkan Sketches

The bus stops
at a scrubby forest edge
about to devour everything.

Slow down.
Look again.
There are people in that rubble.

A Roma girl,
hair as dark as night,
eyes the color of hope.

Among the ice cream vendors and
peddlers of water and soda all
along the Danube;
a fire, unquenchable.

Crossings

We cross the border from Hungary into Serbia. The freight cars in the train yard, stenciled in Cyrillic. The graffiti reads "Fuck U.S." "Fuck NATO."

We have been at the Subotica border crossing for an hour. Outside a steady rain falls. People are taken off the train, hauling their luggage through the wet to a shabby old building by the side of the tracks.

Nobody asks me a thing. I am invisible. There is much I do not understand.

A whistle. The train creaks to life.

A middle-aged woman in working-class blue moves through the car, emptying garbage mechanically, as if we weren't even there, as if she didn't care if you saw her or not. There is little warmth in her, little human about her movements, her manner, not even her dark, girlish ponytail.

A teenage girl across the aisle sits oblivious to the woman collecting garbage. The soft thump of Balkan pop leaks from her white earbuds. Her pink toenails tap the dull steel footrest, pink fingernails delicately press buttons on her bejeweled mobile phone.

A fire burns by the side of the tracks. Night is falling.

Austria-Hungary

Fields of windmills stretch far into the horizon along what was the old Austro-Hungarian border.

Passing through the vast plains of Hungary. Fields of sunflowers, a yellow blanket on a scorched and parched landscape.

Flatness as far as the eye can see. Rolled bales of hay lounge in empty fields. Off in the distance, the silhouette of a factory, smokestacks like dark barcode lines.

The endless countryside in its black widow's dress.

The black dog, the crumbling white house.

Budapest

The museum of the Cold War.

Sections of the old electric fence that once ran the length of the Austrian border. Old street signs with Lenin, Marx, and Engels crossed out. Hammer and sickles cut out from the center of the Hungarian flag.

A six-foot statue of Stalin pointing off into the distance, smiling youth surrounding him. Girls carrying bundles of healthy wheat, red-starred flags flapping happily in the breeze of a glorious new human future.

By the Danube, a Burger King, its dining room walls lined with prints of American life—a baseball, a cowgirl neon sign from Vegas, a New York City taxi cab, a diner bathed in cool blue light, the word HOT in red neon, a hand on a football about to be snapped, a Route 66 sign.

At Keleti station, crumbling facades, crooked chimneys, missing shingles.

In the twilight, ads for escorts on streetlights, flickering to life.

Acknowledgements

Gratitude to the editors of the following publications where these poems first appeared:

Poetrybay: "Four Balkan Sketches"
The Long Islander: "Cheyenne"
The City Poetry: "The City"
Gasconade Review: "Ode to the Hermit Crab"

"Breakfast at a Boston McDonald's" —Previously published in *Rustbelt Romance* (deep cleveland press)

"The Traveler"—Previously published in *Departures* (Burning River Press)

45TH PARALLEL

AS YOU STAND HERE, YOU ARE HALFWAY BETWEEN THE EQUATOR AND THE NORTH POLE

MILENKO (MILES) BUDIMIR is the author of several books of poems including *Licorice Heart* (Roadside Press), *Departures* (Burning River) and *Rustbelt Romance* (deep cleveland). His photographs have appeared in numerous exhibitions over the years where they have won awards and been acquired for private collections. He works as a philosophy lecturer and a technical writer and editor. He is from Cleveland, Ohio.

MORE ROADSIDE PRESS TITLES

MORE ROADSIDE PRESS TITLES

MORE ROADSIDE PRESS TITLES

MORE ROADSIDE PRESS TITLES

Collected Poems
(2005-2025)
Michele McDannold

The Work Anxiety Poems
Alan Catlin